Why Does the Change in Shares Predict Stock Returns?

Introduction

The stock of firms that repurchase equity has, in the years after the equity activity,

outperformed the stock of firms with no change in shares. In turn, the stock of firms with no

change in shares has done better than the stock of firms that issue equity. Nelson (1999)

presents evidence that these excess returns are large, statistically significant, and persist after

controlling for market risk. Similarly, Loughran and Ritter (1995) find the stock of firms that

engage in seasoned equity offerings tends to perform poorly over the following five years,

and Ikenberry, Lakonishok and Vermaelen (1995) document that the stock of firms

repurchasing shares tends to do well. The excess returns are measured after the equity

activity becomes public and are thus distinct from any effect on the stock price of the

announcement of the change in shares.[2] One explanation offered by these studies for the

excess returns is that firms are exploiting their superior knowledge about the value of their

stock by buying it when it is undervalued and selling it when it is overvalued. In this paper I

present supporting evidence for this explanation of the excess returns.

Of course, firms issue and repurchase equity for reasons that have nothing to do with

the value of their equity. In general, if a firm wants to get bigger it has an incentive to raise

funds on all margins, including by issuing equity, while a firm that wants to get smaller has

---

2. The announcement effects go in the same direction as the anomalous holding returns: the stock
price jumps upon announcement of a repurchase, falls upon announcement of an issue. Dann (1981),
Masulis (1980), Rosenfeld (1982), and Vermaelen (1981, 1984) examine abnormal returns around
repurchase tender offers. Asquith and Mullins (1986), Masulis and Korwar (1986) and Mikkelson and
Partch (1986) examine abnormal returns around the announcement of a new issue of common stock.

the incentive to repurchase its equity. Holding the size of the firm constant, a firm likely has an incentive to issue or repurchase shares to adjust to its equilibrium capital structure. A firm that is highly levered may want to issue equity while a firm with low leverage may want to repurchase equity.

The influence of equity valuation enters the decision to issue or repurchase through the relative cost of the firms' sources of finance. One definition of a deviation of stock price from fundamental value is that the stock is currently overvalued if the expected returns to investing in it are lower than appropriate given its level of risk (negative excess returns) and undervalued if it offers higher returns than appropriate for its level of risk (positive excess returns). This would be the relationship between deviation of fundamental value and excess returns if the stock price were expected to return to its fundamental value over time, adding a negative component to the expected returns of an overvalued firm, and a positive component to the expected returns of an undervalued firms.[3]

A firm wishing to raise funds likely evaluates the expense of all of its sources, exploiting those which appear cheapest. If it judges the expected returns inherent in its stock price, taking into account any expected announcement effect upon issuance, to be below its other funding options, it will raise money by issuing stock. Similarly, a firm which judges its stock to offer higher returns than its other investment options, even after the stock rose upon announcement of a tender offer, would repurchase.

---

3. The relationship would also obtain weakly if the deviations were expected to be permanent, since dividend yields would be high for an undervalued firm and low for an overvalued firm. If the deviations were the results of rational bubbles (which can only support positive deviations), where the expected loss is offset by expected continued capital gains, there would be no relationship between deviations and expected excess returns.

As long as equity valuation influences some firms' decisions to issue or repurchase, the change in shares will be correlated with stock returns even though much of the change in shares occurs for reasons independent of valuation issues. A portfolio of issuers, for example, would contain a greater-than-typical percentage of overvalued firms and would therefore generate low average subsequent returns.

This explanation for the excess returns has several other implications. First, the change in shares outstanding should be positively correlated with measures of stock price deviation from fundamental value at the time of issue or repurchase. One proxy for deviation from fundamental value is the ratio of the book value to the market value of equity, which Fama and French (1992) show is strongly positively related to subsequent stock returns. Another proxy is suggested by the work of Lakonishok, Shleifer, and Vishny (1994). They identify firms which have experienced rapid sales growth over recent years and are expected to perform well in the future, which they label glamor stocks, and firms that have experienced slow sales growth and are expected to perform poorly in the future, which they label value stocks. They document that the glamor stocks tend to underperform and value stocks tend to overperform. As shown below, the correlation of the change in shares outstanding with both of these measures suggests overvalued firms are more likely to issue and undervalued firms more likely to repurchase. The correlations remain significant even after controlling for firms' leverage and rate of investment in plant and equipment.

The second implication is that the excess returns following the change in shares should remain significant after controlling for these proxies for the deviation of stock price from fundamental value; that is, because the proxies are imperfect measures, the change in shares

3

should have power to predict that part of excess returns not captured by the proxies. I find that the change in shares remains significant after controlling for these proxies, and, in fact, slightly outperforms the other measures.[4] Again, this result continues to hold after controlling for firms' rate of investment and leverage.

The third and final implication explored here is that changes in shares that can be explained by proxies for deviations from fundamental value should predict stock returns more powerfully than changes in shares explained by other reasons. When the change in shares is decomposed into a component explained by the proxies and a component explained by investment and leverage, the former predicts excess returns that are about two and one half times the size of those predicted by the latter. As a closely related aside to this final implication, I also present some evidence that the equity activity in response to deviations from fundamental value appear to influence the capital investment decisions of corporations.

In a recently published paper, Loughran and Ritter (1997) examine the operating performance of firms that conduct seasoned equity offers. They find that firms that issue stock have, on average, experienced an improvement in profitability and an increase in market-to-book ratios in the years proceeding the issue, and that both of these measures deteriorate following the issue. They also find that while high-growth firms tend to experience worse subsequent stock performance than low-growth firms, firms that issue stock do worse than those that do not issue, even after controlling for growth.

The organization of the rest of the paper is as follows: The second section describes

---

4. Loughran and Ritter (1995) also show that the under-performance of stock after a seasoned issuance can not be explained by firms' book-to-market ratios.

the data. The third section examines the correlation of the change in shares with firm characteristics. The fourth section examines the predictive power for stock returns of the change in shares after controlling for firm characteristics. The fifth section examines the predictive power of the components of the change in shares, and the final section concludes.

The data

The analysis requires information on the change in shares outstanding, stock returns, and balance sheet and income data. The data are from the December 1997 Center for Research in Security Prices (CRSP) stock file and the May 1998 COMPUSTAT database. The CRSP database includes information on all securities traded on the NYSE, AMEX and Nasdaq exchanges. The change in shares outstanding and the stock return are from the CRSP file. The change in shares is corrected for splits and stock dividends. In order to be included in the sample, the securities must have at least one year of complete data. Missing observations of a single month of returns were interpolated, but securities with two successive months of missing returns were excluded. When securities were delisted, any final disbursement was included as the last return and returns to the end of the year were calculated using an equally weighted index of the securities in the database.[5] These criteria selected over 17,000 securities from the 21,500 in the database, with the most common reason for exclusion being data for an insufficient length of time to calculate a change in shares.

Data on these securities were then matched by firm and security identifying numbers

---

5. This procedure allows for the collection of data at an annual frequency, while at the same time reproducing the returns available to a feasible investment strategy.

(CUSIP) to the data on corporate balance sheet and income data on publicly traded corporations in the COMPUSTAT database. The COMPUSTAT data are for 1978 to 1997. Matching by CUSIP identified COMPUSTAT data for 85 percent of the securities selected from CRSP that had data during the relevant time interval. The final dataset has 95,000 firm-year observations. The data selected from COMPUSTAT include the book value of equity, the market value of equity, sales, net income before extraordinary items, depreciation, investment in plant and equipment, the stock of plant and equipment, and total assets. These variables are used to form the book-to-market ratio, the ratio of cash flow (net income plus depreciation) to market value, the capital investment rate (investment in plant and equipment divided by the lagged capital stock), and the ratio of book equity to assets as an (inverse) measure of leverage.

Lakonishok et al (1994) emphasize that the glamor or value of a stock is best evaluated by combining a measure of past performance with an indicator of expected future performance. They find that the growth in sales and the ratio of cash flow to market value is the combination among those they consider that best predicts future stock returns. A low cash flow to market value ratio is taken as indicative of high expected future growth in cash flow, since the high price of the stock suggests investors believe profitability will improve. They identify as glamor (overvalued) stocks those of firms that had done well recently (rapid growth in sales) and were expected to do well in the future (low ratio of cash flow to market value) and these stock subsequently performed poorly. Value stocks, which performed well, were identified as those that had experienced low sales growth and had a high ratio of cash flow to market value.

I measure growth in sales in the same manner as Lakonishok et al. For each year annual sales growth is ranked across firms.[6] The weighted average rank over the past five years is then constructed placing a weight of five on the current year and using linearly declining weights ending with a weight of one on the rank four years back.[7] Since it requires five consecutive years of data to calculate the growth in sales rank, the sample shrinks appreciably (by more than half) when this variable is included.

In order to identify a single measure on the value-glamor scale I first order the firms by their five-year sales rank and separately by their ratio of cash flow to market value, identifying for each the top and bottom thirty percent of observations each year. Combining these rankings yields five possible combinations, which I then normalize so that 1 equals value and 5 equals glamor. This technique provides a single index of the value-glamor characteristics of a stock at the expense of imposing equal weights on the importance of sales growth and the ratio of cash flow to market value.[8]

Table 1 includes a description of the variables used in the analysis. To help clarify the timing of the variables, a time line has also been included at the bottom of table 1. The change in shares is always calculated from December to December. The firm characteristics are for fiscal year end (for balance sheet items) or the fiscal year (for income and expense

---

6. Although Lakonishok et al are not clear on this point, I give each firm a percentage rank rather than an absolute rank, to avoid the average rank being a function of the number of observations in a given year.

7. Lakonishok et al report that their results are similar when the annual sales ranks are equally weighted when calculating the average rank.

8. Lakonishock et all use the same percentage cutoffs in their analysis. They do not, however, combine the results in a single index.

items) and are identified by the year containing the fiscal year end. For example, a balance sheet item is treated as coincident with the change in shares if it is from the fiscal year that ends in the calendar year of the change in shares, regardless of what month the fiscal year ends. The results presented below are robust to including only those observations (about half) with fiscal years that end in December. The stock returns are calculated from the end of April of the year after the change in shares. This gap ensures the firm characteristics were known at the initiation of the calculation of the returns. In considering reasons why firms buy or sell shares, some of the firm characteristics are lagged one year so that they reflect conditions at the initiation of the change in shares outstanding rather than responses to the change in shares.

Table 2 presents some descriptive statistics. To reduce the influence of outliers the top and bottom one-half percentile of the growth in shares outstanding and of the financial ratios are replaced with the one-half percentile cutoff. The first column reports the sample means and the second column reports the means after the adjustment of the outliers. As can be seen, the inclusion of the outliers can have a profound effect on the estimates of the means of the variables that require correction, and the means are much more plausible after the outliers are removed. The one-half percentile cutoff was chosen as small enough to not significantly influence the basic results, but large enough to catch those few observations which could have a disproportionate impact. By setting the outliers equal to the one-half percentiles rather than removing them, the observations are not lost to the analysis. As discussed in Appendix A, the results reported below are not significantly influenced by the handling of the outliers.

In order to allow for a nonparametric characterization of the data, some of the analysis below divides the data on the change in shares into quintiles.[9] For each year of the sample, firms are sorted into quintiles by the change in shares. The lowest quintile ranking corresponds to the repurchase of equity and the highest to the issuance of equity. The quintiles are formed annually to remove any changes in the aggregate tendencies of firms to repurchase or issue equity. The second page of table 2 presents the average change in shares and average log of market value by quintile. Overall, shares outstanding increased by about 5 percent each year. The average change in shares is negative--indicating a repurchase of shares--only in the bottom quintile. The fraction of firms that experienced negative changes in shares varies between about 16 and 26 percent each year, thus only the bottom quintile typically contains firms that repurchase equity. Between 8 and 23 percent experience no change in shares, and between 60 and 70 percent register an increase. As can be seen in the table, the average change in shares varies little over the middle quintiles, with only the top quintile showing a significant--25 percent--increase.

The change in shares and firm characteristics

Table 3 presents the average characteristics of firms across the change-in-shares quintiles. The first line shows the average lagged book-to-market ratios of the firm-years falling into each quintile. A low book-to-market ratio may suggest overvaluation and a high book-to-market ratio undervaluation. The average book-to-market ratios fall monotonically

---

9. This procedure also has the advantage of being robust to problems caused by outliers in the variable used to form the quintiles.

across the change in shares quintiles, as would be the case if firms tended to repurchase undervalued stock and issue overvalued stock. In total, the average book-to-market ratio declines by 35 percentage points between the lowest and highest change in shares quintiles, about one half of the standard deviation of the book-to-market ratio after removing the outliers.

The next line shows the average of the value-glamor index of the firm-years. The average rankings also vary across change-in-shares quintiles in a manner suggesting firms are repurchasing undervalued and selling overvalued stock. The average index rises by one-half rank between the lowest and the highest change in shares quintile. The components of the index--the ratio of cash flow to market value and the average growth in sales rank--also vary across the change-in-shares quintiles in a way consistent with the hypothesis that firms repurchase undervalued and sell overvalued stock. The better the firm's past performance or expected future performance, the greater the issuance of stock.

Lakonishok et al (1994) report that it is important to combine the information in sales growth and the ratio of cash flow to market value when identifying value or glamor stocks. Therefore, there may be some value to considering the value-glamor index rather than the sales growth and cash flow to market value components separately. Furthermore, firms with rapidly growing sales are also likely to be expanding and therefore issuing stock to fund capital investment. If sales growth were included as a separate explanatory variable for the change in shares, it would be unclear if it were measuring firms' need to expand or deviations of stock price from fundamental value. Firms with low ratios of cash flow to market value also likely often have low book-to-market ratios, so the ratio of cash flow to market value may not, by itself, contain much information about deviations from fundamental value. Combining the growth in sales and the ratio of cash flow to market value into a single index may better identify an independent proxy for deviations of stock price from fundamentals and an independent factor influencing firms decisions to issue or repurchase equity.

Other firm characteristics also vary across change-in-shares quintiles as expected. The investment rate for the fiscal year of the change in shares is included as the measure of firms' growth-related need for finance. Firms in the highest quintile have, on average, investment rates double those of the firms in the lowest quintile. Book equity as a percentage of assets measures financing-related incentives to issue or repurchase equity. Firms with a high ratio have low leverage and may therefore be more likely to repurchase equity. The lowest change in shares quintile does have the lowest average ratio of book equity to assets, and the highest change in shares quintile has the highest average ratio. However, the average ratio of book equity to assets does not vary much and does not decline monotonically across the quintiles.

Because over or undervaluation generally implies excess returns only if the valuation levels tend to revert to normal, the observation that firms that issue stock have low book-to-market ratios and those that repurchase stock have high book-to-market ratios is not sufficient to explain the excess returns: the differences in book-to-market ratios should go away over time. The bottom three lines show the average book-to-market ratios of firms by change-in-shares quintiles the year before, the year of, and five years after the change in shares. Only firms that survive five years after the change in shares are included in the sample. Over the six years, the difference between the book-to-market ratios of the bottom and top quintiles declines from nearly 30 percentage points to 11 percentage points.[10]

Table 4 contains the results of regressions of the change in shares on the firm characteristics. The regressions include year dummies to control for aggregate changes (not shown), and the log of market value to control for the effects of firm size. As shown in the first line, the change in shares is negatively related to firm size. The book-to-market ratio, added in the second line, is significantly negatively correlated with the change in shares, but the coefficient estimate suggests a fairly small effect. Increasing a firm's book-to-market ratio by one standard deviation reduces the predicted change in shares by 15 percent of one standard deviation of the change in shares. Similarly, the value-glamor index is significantly positively related to the change in shares, but each step in the index (which equals one standard deviation) corresponds to only a 1-1/3 percentage point increase in the change in shares (less than 10 percent of one standard deviation of the change in shares). When entered jointly, both measures of potential deviations from fundamental value remain significant with similar coefficients, suggesting independent information in the two measures on the incentives to repurchase or issue equity.

The change in shares is significantly positively correlated with the investment rate and negatively correlated with the ratio of book equity to assets. Again, the coefficients suggest modest effects: Each one percentage point increase in the investment rate corresponds to a 0.03 percentage point increase in shares outstanding. A firm with one percentage point higher

---

10. Survivorship bias does not seem to be generating this result. When all firms with a current and lagged value are included and the book-to-market ratios five years ahead are set equal to the observation furthest into the future (up to five years) available, the spread between the book-to-market ratios of the bottom and top quintiles declines from 36 percentage points to 19 percentage points, essentially the same narrowing of the spread as when only the survivors are included.

than average book equity increases its shares by 0.06 percentage points less than average.

The results remain similar and significant when all of the firm characteristics are included together, suggesting each is measuring a somewhat independent reason why firms issue and repurchase. These conclusions also hold for the most economically significant firms: As shown in the bottom line, when the sample is restricted to the largest half of firms, the estimated coefficients retain their sign, significance, and general magnitude.[11]

Portfolio returns of change-in-shares quintiles, controlling for deviations from fundamental value

The results in the preceding section suggest that firms that issue and repurchase equity do so, to some extent, when their stock appears over or under valued by measures that are correlated with future excess returns. While this result lends support to the view that firms are reacting to their perceptions about the value of their stock, it also raises the possibility that the excess returns following the share activity are a manifestation of the book-to-market or value-glamor stock market anomalies. A natural question is whether changes in shares forecast excess returns even controlling for these measures of stock price deviation from fundamentals.

The results shown in table 5 support the idea that there is additional information in the

---

11. However, there is a complex relationship between firm size, change in shares, and book-to-market ratio. As firm size increases, average change in shares declines, the average book-to-market ratio declines, and the sensitivity of the change in shares to the book-to-market ratio declines. This relationship appears to be well captured by adding an interaction term of the log market value times the book-to-market ratio. Nevertheless, since the results reported here are essentially unchanged when an interaction term is included, and adding the term complicates the exposition, I do not include the interaction term.

change in shares. The top panel shows the annualized, five-year holding returns for portfolios of stocks grouped by book-to-market ratio and by the change in shares. Each year, firms are sorted by their fiscal-year-end book-to-market ratio and grouped into quintiles. Within each of these quintiles the firms are sorted by their December-to-December change in shares outstanding from the year that contains the fiscal-year end observation on the book-to-market ratio. The equally-weighted five-year holding returns are then calculated for each of the resulting twenty-five portfolios starting at the end of April in the year following the formation of the portfolios. When a stock is delisted before the end of the five-year period, any proceeds are invested in the remaining firms in the portfolio.[12] The figures shown in the top half of the table are the average returns for the fourteen portfolios, one each for 1978 to 1991, falling into each cell. The bottom half (which requires the five-year growth in sales) reports the average over the 9 portfolios formed between 1983 and 1991.

As can be seen by comparing the return on the highest and lowest change-in-shares quintiles across the book-to-market quintiles, controlling for the book-to-market ratio does not remove the difference in ex-post return between those firms that repurchase and those that issue equity. The return on firms in the lowest change-in-shares quintile exceeds the return on those in the highest by between 5 and 10 percent per-year. On average, the difference in returns was 8-1/2 percent, only a bit below the average difference of 11 percent with no control for book-to-market ratios (shown at the bottom).

The negative correlation between a firms' book-to-market ratio and its subsequent

---

12. As discussed in the data section, when stocks are delisted during the year, any remaining proceeds are invested in the equally-weighted market index through the end of the year, allowing for the treatment of the data at an annual frequency. When calculating the portfolio returns, the proceeds at the end of the year are then reinvested in the remaining stocks in the portfolio.

stock returns is also evident. A portfolio of firms that had high book-to-market ratios and repurchased their own stock posted annual returns 36 percentage points greater, on average, than a portfolio of low book-to-market stock issuers.

The bottom panel shows the results when the stocks are first sorted by the value-glamor index rather than their book-to-market quintile. Again, the average returns generally decline across the change-in-shares quintiles even after controlling for the value-glamor index, except for the most glamorous firms, for which the highest returns are on the middle change-in-shares quintile. For all levels of the value-glamor index, however, the return on the lowest change in shares quintile is well in excess of the return on the highest quintile. The difference in the average return across change-in-shares portfolios is about 7 percentage points, and the average difference between the best (value firms that repurchase stock) and worst (glamor firms that issue stock) performing portfolios is 24 percentage points.[13]

Stock returns, the change in shares, and firm characteristics

In order to evaluate the statistical significance of the differences in returns, as well as to control for other reasons to issue or repurchase, I estimate regressions of ex-post firm returns on firm characteristics. Following Fama-MacBeth (1973), cross-sectional regressions are estimated for each year of the sample. The coefficients are then averaged across years and the t-statistics are the ratio of this estimate of the mean to its time-series standard error.

---

13. Although these results reflect an implementable investment strategy, lost observations owing to incomplete data may raise concerns that the differences in returns reported here may not be robust to including a less exclusive panel of stocks. The differences in returns reported in Nelson (1999), for which complete data on the change in shares outstanding is the sole requirement for inclusion in the portfolios, are similar to those reported here.

This procedure ensures that all information used to predict returns is available before the calculation of the returns. This procedure also correctly accounts for the fact that the regression is based on a moment condition over time, not across firms. Specifically, the regression is testing a hypothesis about the expected returns on the stock of firms with given characteristics, not the cross section of returns. For example, consider evaluating the hypothesis that the expected returns are a function of the commodity-price sensitivity of each corporation's earnings. Since commodity prices vary, the cross-section of ex-post returns in any given year will likely be significantly related to the corporations' earnings sensitivity, even though the expected returns may be completely unrelated to the sensitivity. Of course, each year the estimated coefficient on the commodity price sensitivity would vary, depending on the actual movement in commodity prices. Over time, if the expected returns are independent of the sensitivity, the estimated coefficients would have an average value insignificantly different from zero. If there were sufficient time periods, the OLS value would also equal zero, but the current sample includes thousands of stocks each year, but only a few years of data. The Fama-MacBeth procedure correctly uses only the across-time degrees of freedom in calculating the t-statistics.

Generally, the dependent variable is the annualized five-year holding return calculated from the April following the year in which the firm characteristics are measured. For those firms that do not survive the full five years, equally-weighted market returns are used to fill in the final observations. All the regressions include the log of the market value of the firm at the end of its fiscal year to control for size effects. Unlike the regressions for the change in shares, none of the firm characteristics are lagged, so that the firm characteristics are not improperly handicapped relative to the change in shares when predicting returns.

Table 6 shows the results when the five-year returns are regressed on the firm characteristics. As a benchmark, shown in the top line, when returns are regressed on only the change in shares and firm size, the estimates suggest that for each percentage point increase in the change in shares, ex-post returns are 31 basis points lower, on average. The estimated effect is highly significant.

As shown in the second line, the estimate is little changed--falling to 24 basis points-- when the book-to-market ratio is included in the regression. The book-to-market ratio also enters significantly, although slightly less so than the change-in-shares. When the value- glamor index is included, the estimated effect of the change in shares drops further, to 15 basis points, but remains highly significant. The coefficients on both the book-to-market ratio and the value-glamor index are significant.

The non-valuation reasons for changes in shares also show some limited predictive power for subsequent returns. When added to the change in shares and firm size, increased capital investment is significantly related to a slight decline in future returns. Capital investment may predict returns because the market overvalues past growth and past growth is likely correlated with capital investment. In addition, firms with overvalued stock have access to a relatively less expensive sources of finance than firms with undervalued stock. The predictive power of the investment variable may reflect the influence of this difference on the cost of capital across firms.

An increase in the ratio of book equity to assets marginally (at the 10 percent level) also predicts slightly lower stock returns. This result may reflect the fact that more highly levered (lower book equity to assets) firms, other things equal, should have riskier stock and therefore have higher average returns.

When all of the variables are included, only the change in shares, the book-to-market ratio, and the value glamor index significantly predict future returns. The proxies for deviation of stock price from fundamentals appear to capture the reasons capital investment and leverage predict returns. When all the firm characteristics are included without the change in shares, shown on the next line, the results are little changed, although the coefficient on the value-glamor index rises somewhat.

As a check on robustness of the estimation technique, the bottom three lines present alternative estimates of the regression that includes all the explanatory variables. When the observations are restricted to the 50 percent of firms each year with the largest market value, the estimates are largely unchanged, except the value-glamor index no longer enters significantly. Estimates using OLS instead of the Fama-MacBeth technique nearly match those using Fama-MacBeth. Finally, it seems possible that the overlapping nature of the five-year returns may impose a false stability over time on the cross-sectional coefficient estimates, biasing the t-statistics toward significance. However, the estimates are also nearly unchanged when the one-year rather than the five-year subsequent returns are the dependent variable, indicating the overlapping observations are not responsible for the significance of the coefficients.[14]

––––––––––––––––––––––

14. Appendix A reports results for several additional specifications of this regression including correction for the serial correlation in the errors, estimation for firms with December-fiscal year ends, and variation in the treatment of outliers. In all cases, the results are little different from those reported here.

Stock returns and the components of the change in shares

If the change in shares predicts stock returns because of opportunistic behavior by firms, the predictive power should be greatest for that part of the change in shares correlated with deviations from fundamental value, and absent for that part correlated with other reasons. In this section, the regression of the change in shares on firm characteristics is used to decompose the change in shares into four components, each of which is used to predict returns. The first component is the fitted value from a regression of the change in shares on firm size, because many of the exogenous variables vary systematically with size in a manner likely to be unrelated to the forces influencing a firm's decision to buy or sell equity. The second component is the fitted value from a regression of the residual from the firm-size regression on the independent-of-size variation in variables that may motivate a firm to issue or repurchase equity that are unrelated to the relative valuation of its stock: the rate of investment during the year of the change in shares, and the lagged ratio of the book value of equity to assets. The third component is the fitted value from a regression of the still unexplained part of the change in shares on lagged measures of deviations from fundamental value: the book-to-market ratio and the value-glamor index, from which have first been removed variation explained by firm size and the non-valuation-related variables. The residual from that regression is the fourth and final component, representing that part of the change in shares explained by none of these variables.

The predictive power of these four components for five-year stock returns is then evaluated using Fama-MacBeth regressions. The results are reported in table 7. As shown in the top line, the results are generally supportive of the view that the excess returns following equity activity are the result of firms exploiting their superior knowledge when buying or selling their own equity. Although all the components except that related to firm size are significantly related to the future stock returns, the coefficient on the fraction of the change in shares related to deviations from fundamental value is more than two and one-half times as large as the coefficient on the change in shares related to non-valuation reasons. The coefficient on the residual component of the change in shares is the smallest of the three significant components.

The residual may be correlated with unmeasured deviations from fundamental value because the proxies for deviation are imperfect, so it is not surprising that the residual change in shares should significantly predict stock returns. What is surprising is that changes in shares explained by investment and leverage predict stock returns.

Since the non-valuation-related variables are given priority in explaining the change in shares, the predictive power of the component of the change in shares explained by investment and leverage may reflect, as discussed above, the stock of firms that are growing rapidly being overvalued and the stock of firms that are not growing being undervalued. This phenomena is precisely what the growth in sales is measuring in the value-glamor index. As shown on the second line, when the proxies for deviation from fundamental value are given priority, the coefficient on and significance of the investment and leverage component do decline slightly, but the coefficient remains highly significant: the non-valuation-related variables do not just appear to be standing in for the valuation proxies.

In the case of the ratio of book equity to assets, it is difficult to explain this result. Firms with a lower ratio of book equity to assets tend to issue shares but also tend to have marginally higher, not lower, average returns. The fraction of the change in shares related to capital investment may predict returns for the reasons investment predicts returns discussed in the previous section: Firms whose stock is overvalued may invest more because they have access to cheaper funds. Firms whose stock is undervalued may invest less, using their funds instead to buy stock.

As shown in the bottom line, when the estimation is limited to the largest firms, the component of the change in shares related to non-valuation variables is insignificantly related to future returns although the component related to the valuation proxies and the residual component both remain significant. Thus, the estimates using the largest firms are more supportive of the view that the predictive power of the change in shares for future returns reflects opportunistic behavior by firms than are the results using the entire sample.

A digression on deviations from fundamental value and capital investment

The issue of whether or not the component of the change in shares explained by capital investment predicts returns is of sufficient importance to give it separate attention. It could be the case that even if corporations issue and repurchase their stock in response to deviations in their stock price from what they judge to be its fundamental value, the corporations' capital investment decisions are unaffected. In this case, the funds raised by an issue or used by a repurchase would be offset exclusively by other liabilities or financial assets.[15] If capital investment is unaffected, noisy stock prices affect only the distribution of financial assets and perhaps not economic welfare.

---

15. Appendix B examines the source or use of funds for share repurchases or issues.

However, the complimentary implication of the hypothesis that capital investment is unaffected is that the change in shares explained by capital investment should not predict stock returns. Table 8 presents the results of Fama-MacBeth regressions for five-year returns using just the change in shares. The first line reports the results when the independent variable is the actual change in shares. The second line reports the results when the independent variable is the fitted values from a regression of the change in shares on the rate of capital investment. The fitted change in shares is highly significant, indicating that the change in shares explained by capital investment does predict returns.[16] As a result, it is almost possible to reject the hypothesis that capital investment is not influenced by deviations of stock prices from fundamental value. It may be, however, that this result reflects, in part, managers and investors holding the same mistaken beliefs about corporations' prospects so that capital investment and deviations from fundamental value are positively correlated even though the deviations have no independent effect on investment.

Conclusion

In summary, the characteristics of firms that issue and repurchase equity suggest the change in shares predicts returns because issuance is encouraged by stock price overvaluation and repurchase by undervaluation. The change in shares outstanding is positively correlated with proxies for stock price deviation from fundamental value. The excess returns following the change in shares remain significant after controlling for these proxies of the deviation of

---

16. Of course, the fitted change in shares is perfectly correlated with the rate of capital investment, so this is just another way to demonstrate that differences in capital investment predict stock returns.

stock price from fundamental value. The changes in shares that can be explained by the proxies predict stock returns more powerfully than changes in shares explained by other variables.

There are at least two reasons why the ability of the change in shares to predict stock returns deserves special attention among stock market anomalies. First, the hypothesis that the change in shares might predict returns follows logically from the possibility that markets are not perfectly efficient. Thus, the finding that the change in shares does, in fact, predict returns is less vulnerable to the fishing-expedition concerns raised with respect to many stock market anomalies. Furthermore, since the change in shares is not a function of the market value of the firm, such as the ratio of book value or earnings to market value, the predictive power can not be generated by equilibrium variation in required returns, a concern raised by Berk (1995).

The second reason the change in shares anomaly deserves attention is that it represents one of the linkages between the stock market and the real economy. One of the ways deviations of stock prices from fundamental value could affect the economy is through firms' capital investment decisions. Indeed, once the predictive power of the change in shares is acknowledged, it is hard to maintain that the stock market does not influence capital investment. To do so is to maintain that issuance and repurchases of equity in response to deviations of stock prices from fundamentals only influence other financial variables. The compliment to this assertion is that issuance and repurchases of equity correlated with capital investment should not predict stock returns--in contradiction to the findings in this paper.

Table 1
Variable Definitions

Variable	Abbreviation	Definition
Change in shares outstanding	Change in Shares	The December-to-December percentage change in shares outstanding corrected for stock splits and stock dividends.
Book-to-market ratio	Book/ Market	The book value of common equity divided by the market value of common equity, in percent. Compustat data items (60/(199*25))*100
Ratio of cash-flow to market value	Cash Flow/ Market	Net income before extraordinary items plus depreciation as a percentage of market value. Compustat data items (18+14)/(199*25)*100
Weighted growth in sales rank	Sales Growth	The five-year weighted average growth in sales (Compustat data item 12) percentage rank. The weights are year t=5 to year t-4=1.
Value-Glamor Rank	Value-Glamor	Index between one and five, where 1 designates firms with slow past sales growth and a high cash flow to market ratio, and 5 designates firms with fast past sales growth and a low cash flow to market ratio.
Capital investment rate	Capital Investment	Ratio of investment in plant and equipment (Compustat data item 30) to lagged stock of plant and equipment (Compustat data item 8), in percent.
Book equity to Assets	Equity/ Assets	Ratio of book value of common stock to total assets (Compustat data item 6), in percent. Note that the greater is this variable, the lower is the firm's leverage.
Log (Market Value)	Market Value	Log of the fiscal-year-end market value in $thousands (Compustat data item 199*25).
Stock returns	Return	Except were noted, the stock returns are the five year holding return, in percent at an annual rate.

(Continued)

Table 1 (cont.)

Time Line

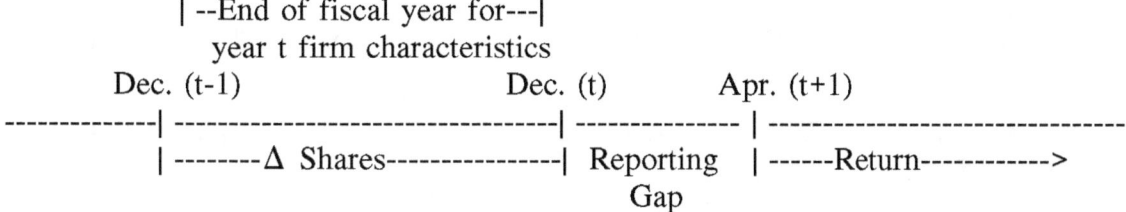

```
          | --End of fiscal year for---|
            year t firm characteristics
       Dec. (t-1)                      Dec. (t)        Apr. (t+1)
--------------| --------------------------------| -------------- | -------------------------------
       | --------Δ Shares----------------| Reporting  | ------Return------------>
                                           Gap
```

25

Table 2
Descriptive Statistics

Variable	Mean (Std. Dev.) Full Sample	Mean (Std. Dev.) No Outliers	Percentiles				
			0.5	10	50	90	99.5
Change in shares	5.05 (18.29)	4.91 (15.25)	-30.0	-1.7	0.5	17.8	416.5
Book/ Market	354.10 (76,955.35)	72.08 (73.24)	-240.3	15.6	59.7	147.4	416.5
Value-Glamor	2.8 (1.06)		1	1	3	4	5
Cash Flow/ Market	8.32 (8,367.95)	3.79 (45.48)	-331.4	-12.4	9.4	25.3	78.3
Sales growth	709.47 (248.80)		150.5	397.9	695.3	1050	1347
Capital Investment	61.13 (906.75)	46.14 (84.70)	0	6.5	24.4	91.6	773.8
Equity/ Assets	42.13 (131.78)	43.77 (28.57)	-82.9	8.0	44.6	80.0	97.2
Market Value	4.24 (2.07)		-0.7	1.7	4.1	7.0	9.9
One-year Return	16.09 (69.61)		-89.1	-45.7	7.2	78.3	319.5
Five-year Return	20.72 (44.89)		-19.8	-14.4	11.9	59.2	241.4

(continued)

Table 2 (cont.)
Descriptive Statistics

Average Within Change-in-Shares Quintiles

	Quintile				
	1	2	3	4	5
Change in shares	-3.08	0.05	0.58	2.89	25.39
Market Value	4.01	3.92	4.74	4.62	4.31

Note: The variables are defined in table 1. The mean and standard deviations in the second column are for the variables with the top and bottom one-half percentile each year set equal to the one-half percentile cutoffs. The percentiles reported in the table are for the entire sample, and thus do not correspond exactly to the annual percentiles used as cutoffs. In the results reported below, this procedure is used to remove the outliers of those variables for which a trimmed mean is reported. The change-in-shares quintiles are formed annually.

Table 3
Average Firm Characteristics
Within Change-in-Shares Quintiles

	Change-in-Shares Quintiles				
	1	2	3	4	5
Proxies for Deviation of Stock Price from Fundamentals					
Book/Market	92.79	80.43	72.77	67.68	58.30
Value(1) v. Glamor(5)	2.66	2.69	2.82	2.94	3.09
Cash Flow/Market	9.96	5.12	9.70	8.66	1.25
Sales Growth	682.06	661.94	732.53	759.94	717.70
Traditional Reasons					
Capital Investment	35.77	39.88	39.95	48.40	69.50
Equity/Assets	46.61	45.37	46.10	45.79	40.54
Other					
Log(Market Value)	4.01	3.92	4.74	4.62	4.31
Book/Market 5 Years After Change in Shares					
Year t-1	96.69	86.38	78.62	74.61	68.01
Year t	96.41	91.43	77.88	72.53	64.89
Year t+5	75.92	74.50	66.59	65.67	64.49

Note: The variables are defined in table 1. The statistic reported in each cell is the mean for all firm-year observations in the indicated change-in-shares quintiles. The change-in-shares quintiles are formed annually. To better measure the conditions resulting in the change in shares, all variables except capital investment are for the fiscal year before the change in shares.

Table 4
Coefficients (t-Statistics) from
Regression of Change in Shares on Firm Characteristics

Intercept	Book Market	Value- Glamor	Capital Invest.	Equity Assets	Market Value	R^2 (# Obs.)
8.52 (65.70)					-0.92 (33.34)	0.03 (76,162)
12.43 (76.76)	-0.03 (39.60)				-1.19 (41.96)	0.05 (73,578)
2.94 (10.80)		1.35 (19.40)			-0.67 (19.41)	0.03 (33,341)
6.06 (18.00)	-0.02 (15.66)	1.05 (14.53)			-0.83 (23.23)	0.04 (33,339)
7.46 (52.73)			0.03 (35.82)		-0.94 (32.39)	0.05 (65,386)
11.63 (68.21)				-0.06 (27.52)	-1.01 (36.31)	0.04 (73,578)
11.81 (64.25)			0.03 (41.70)	-0.09 (36.53)	-1.01 (35.13)	0.07 (65,355)
9.10 (25.90)	-0.01 (11.29)	1.22 (16.42)	0.03 (20.61)	-0.10 (30.92)	-0.94 (25.85)	0.09 (30,611)
Top 50 Percent of Firms Each Year by Market Value						
12.60 (24.21)	-0.01 (5.50)	0.77 (8.74)	0.04 (20.34)	-0.10 (25.58)	-1.30 (23.40)	0.10 (18,723)

Note: The variables are defined in table 1. To better measure the conditions resulting in the change in shares, all variables except capital investment are for the fiscal year before the change in shares. Year dummies, restricted to sum to zero, are included in the regressions but not reported.

Table 5
Five-Year Ex-Post Return (Annual Rate)
Portfolios Formed by Change-in-Shares Quintiles
Within Book-to-Market Quintiles or Value-Glamor Rank

	Change-in-Shares Quintiles				
	1	2	3	4	5
Book-to-Market Quintile	5-Year Return (Percent, AR)				
1	14.30	11.29	12.88	8.60	3.94
2	21.92	17.86	21.56	20.67	14.26
3	27.41	22.98	24.20	25.21	18.63
4	31.50	25.36	30.29	28.64	25.26
5	39.72	37.21	28.82	33.82	30.60
Value-Glamor Rank					
1 (Value)	28.75	22.55	20.14	21.80	17.09
2	23.56	18.46	19.11	20.92	16.87
3	18.24	14.70	16.12	17.30	15.45
4	18.86	14.05	18.08	17.53	13.36
5 (Glamor)	12.94	10.49	17.46	4.96	4.49
Memo: Portfolios just based on change in shares					
	27.38	20.98	24.78	24.00	16.45

Note: The variables are defined in table 1. Each year, firms are separated into quintiles based on their fiscal-year-end book-to-market ratio, and within those quintiles, the firms are divided into quintiles based on the change in shares over the calendar year that contains the fiscal-year end book-to-market observation. Twenty-five portfolios are formed using these two rankings, and the five-year holding return is calculated beginning at the end of April in the following year. The returns are annualized by dividing by five. A similar procedure is followed for the value-glamor rank.

Table 6
Average Slopes (t-Statistics) from Annual Regressions of Five-Year Stock Returns on Change in Shares and Selected Firm Characteristics

Intercept	Change in Shares	Book Market	Value-Glamor	Capital Invest.	Equity Assets	Log (Market)
24.23	-0.31					-0.13
(4.46)	(5.59)					(0.22)
14.48	-0.24	0.07				0.56
(3.22)	(5.92)	(4.95)				(1.09)
14.68	-0.15	0.03	-1.08			0.74
(6.31)	(4.63)	(4.98)	(2.58)			(1.93)
24.00	-0.31			-0.03	-0.02	0.05
(4.18)	(5.13)			(3.33)	(1.67)	(0.09)
16.11	-0.16	0.03	-1.24	-0.00	-0.00	0.58
(5.33)	(5.05)	(5.33)	(2.99)	(0.55)	(0.34)	(1.35)
17.03		0.02	-1.46	-0.01	-0.00	0.53
(5.69)		(5.39)	(3.44)	(1.12)	(0.35)	(1.23)
Top 50 Percent of Firms Each Year by Market Value						
15.03	-0.19	0.04	-0.69	0.01	-0.02	0.57
(4.55)	(6.29)	(2.92)	(1.46)	(0.70)	(0.93)	(1.37)
OLS, All Firm-Years						
16.32	-0.14	0.03	-1.04	-0.00	-0.00	0.34
(12.89)	(5.72)	(8.08)	(3.58)	(0.46)	(0.37)	(2.54)
One Year Returns, Average of Annual Regressions						
19.58	-0.19	0.03	-1.31	-0.01	-0.01	-0.32
(2.95)	(3.33)	(1.58)	(1.73)	(2.08)	(0.21)	(0.38)

Note: The variables are defined in table 1. Except where noted, the dependent variable is the five-year ex-post return (percent, AR) calculated from the end of April in the year following the change in shares and firm characteristics. The statistics reported are the average coefficients from annual cross-sectional regressions and the t-statistic is the average slope divided by its time-series standard error. For each specification, the final cross-sectional regression is for 1991, (allowing the calculation of the five-year returns, ending in April 1996) (except for the one-year-return regression, for which the final cross section is 1995). The first cross section depends on data availability and varies from 1978 to 1983. The later date reflects the requirement that five years of sales growth are necessary to calculate the value-glamor index.

Table 7
Average Slopes (t-Statistics) from Annual Regressions of
Five-Year Stock Returns on Decomposition of Change in Shares

Order of Decomposition	Explanatory Variable for Change in Shares			
	Size Log(Market Value)	Traditional: Investment, Equity/Assets	Stock Price Deviations from Fundamentals: Book/Market, Value-Glamor	Residual
Size, Traditional, Deviations From Fundamentals	-0.51 (0.66)	-0.52 (4.58)	-1.31 (3.02)	-0.15 (3.37)
Size, Deviations From Fundamentals, Traditional	-0.48 (0.64)	-0.40 (3.78)	-1.52 (3.87)	-0.15 (3.36)
Top 50 Percent of Firms Each Year by Market Value				
Size, Traditional, Deviations From Fundamentals	-0.58 (1.34)	-0.26 (1.25)	-1.77 (3.33)	-0.17 (3.75)

Note: The variables are defined in table 1. To better measure the conditions resulting in the change in shares, market value, equity/assets, book/market, and value-glamor are lagged one year. The dependent variable is the five-year ex-post return (percent, AR) calculated from the end of April in the year following the change in shares and firm characteristics. The independent variables are a decomposition of the change in shares into components explained by the listed variables. The statistics reported are the average coefficients from annual cross-sectional regressions and the t-statistic is the average slope divided by its time-series standard error. For each specification, the final cross-sectional regression is for 1991, (allowing the calculation of the five-year returns ending in April 1996). The first cross section is for 1984, reflecting the requirement that five years of sales growth are necessary to calculate the value-glamor index and the fact that the value-glamor index is lagged one year.

Table 8

Average Slopes (t-Statistics) from Annual Regressions of
Five-Year Stock Returns on Change in Shares Explained by Capital Investment

	Intercept	Change in Shares
Actual Change in Shares	22.14	-0.35
	(6.38)	(4.48)
Change in Shares Predicted by Capital Investment	27.59	-1.82
	(6.03)	(3.80)

Note: The variables are defined in table 1. The dependent variable is the five-year ex-post return (percent, AR) calculated from the end of April in the year following the change in shares and firm characteristics. The independent variables are the change in shares and the change in shares predicted by a regression of the change in shares on a constant and the rate of capital investment. The statistics reported are the average coefficients from annual cross-sectional regressions and the t-statistic is the average slope divided by its time-series standard error. For each specification, the final cross-sectional regression is for 1991, (allowing the calculation of the five-year returns, ending in April 1996). The first cross section is for 1979.

Appendix A: Alternative estimates of the returns regression

Table A1 presents alternative estimates of the regression of five-year stock returns on the change in shares and firm characteristics. The top line of table A1, which is identical to the bottom line of table 6, shows the regression results using the Fama-MacBeth estimation procedure. The coefficients are the time-series average of annual cross-sectional regression and the t-statistics are the ratio of the time-series average to its time-series standard error.

The second two lines on the table present the estimates using firms with December fiscal year ends, and nonfinancial firms (firms with SIC codes that do not begin with "6"). In both cases, the results are quite similar to those for the whole sample.

The next two lines address the issue of the the overlapping observations for the five-year returns. The overlap may cause the cross-sectional coefficient estimates to be serially correlated over time, biasing the t-stastics. If the independent variables were not varying, and if the sample were not varying, the errors in estimating the coefficients would follow an MA(4) process with linearly-declining weights. The actual error process is more complicated since the independent variables and the sample of firms vary over time. However, the error process is probably fairly well approximated by an AR(1), and the first set of estimates correct the standard error estimates for AR(1) serial correlation. The resulting t-statistics are slightly lower than in the baseline case, but the results are overall basically unchanged.

The second line corrects for the overlap by dividing the firms up randomly into five groups and using each group in sequence for the annual cross-sectional regressions. This way there is no overlap, so the serial correlation induced by the firm-specific shocks is eliminated. Again, the results are basically unaffected. Note, however, that this technique does not correct for serial correlation caused by systematic shocks to the ex-post returns. For example, if interest rates declined sharply one year, leverage may influence the five-year returns in a similar way for all five years that contain the year of the decline.

The final line is the result when the coefficients are chosen to minimize the absolute value of the errors, rather than the squared errors. This technique is much less sensitive to outliers than OLS. The results are quite similar to the baseline case, although the t-statistics are much larger. The t-statistics are overstated since they are estimated from the entire sample simultaneously.

Table A2 presents results for the baseline returns regression when the treatment of outliers is varied. The top line again reproduces the treatment in the text where for those variables subject to outliers--the book-to-market ratio, capital investment, and the equity-to-asset ratio--the entries in excess of the top and bottom one-half percentile each year are set equal to the one-half percentile. The second line reports the results when the outliers are included unmodified. The inclusion of the outliers does not change the basic result--the change in shares, the book-to-market ratio, and the value-glamor index are significantly correlated with future returns. However, the coefficient on the change in shares and the book-to-market ratio fall somewhat and the coefficient on the value-glamor index (which is not subject to outliers since it only varies from 1 to 5) rises. When the outliers are excluded from the analysis, the coefficient on the change in shares rises slightly relative to the base case and the coefficient on the value-glamor index falls slightly. Overall, the treatment of outliers does not change the basic result by much, although the change in the coefficients across the specifications suggest the outliers appear to add noise rather than information to the analysis.

Table A1

Average Slopes (t-Statistics) from Annual Regressions of
Five-Year Stock Returns on Change in Shares and Selected Firm Characteristics
Additional Alternative Specifications

Intercept	Change in Shares	Book Market	Value-Glamor	Capital Invest.	Equity Assets	Log (Market)
Baseline: Fama-MacBeth, all Firms						
16.11	-0.16	0.03	-1.24	-0.00	-0.00	0.58
(5.33)	(5.05)	(5.33)	(2.99)	(0.55)	(0.34)	(1.35)
December Fiscal Year Ends						
15.43	-0.12	0.03	-1.07	-0.02	0.01	0.54
(3.85)	(3.97)	(3.89)	(1.86)	(2.16)	(0.62)	(1.15)
Nonfinancial Firms						
16.11	-0.16	0.03	-1.24	-0.00	-0.00	0.58
(5.33)	(5.05)	(5.33)	(2.99)	(0.55)	(0.34)	(1.35)
Coefficient t-Statistics Corrected for AR(1)						
16.52	-0.16	0.03	-1.34	-0.01	-0.00	0.64
(4.01)	(4.20)	(6.03)	(2.21)	(0.59)	(0.32)	(0.87)
Firms Used Every Fifth Year to Avoid Overlap						
10.40	-0.18	0.04	-0.97	0.03	-0.00	1.10
(3.32)	(5.17)	(4.31)	(1.50)	(1.56)	(0.32)	(2.34)
Median Regression						
5.25	-0.13	0.03	-1.94	-0.01	-0.02	1.81
(6.25)	(8.17)	(11.19)	(10.23)	(2.59)	(1.84)	(20.47)

Note: The variables are defined in table 1. The dependent variable is the five-year ex-post return (percent, AR) calculated from the end of April in the year following the change in shares and firm characteristics. The statistics reported for the Fama-MacBeth specification are the average coefficients from the nine annual cross-sectional regressions between 1983 and 1991 and the t-statistics are the average slopes divided by their time-series standard error. The results for firms with December fiscal year ends and for nonfinancial firms use the Fama-MacBeth estimation technique for the specified subset of firms. The results with the coefficients corrected for an AR(1) correct the time-series standard errors of the estimates of the average slopes for the serial correlation caused by the overlap in the five-year returns. The results for firms used only every fifth year mitigate the bias induced by the overlap by using only one fifth of the firms each year. The median regression results minimize the mean absolute deviation and are therefore insensitive to outliers, but since they are estimated for the entire sample simultaneously, the t-statistics are upwardly biased.

Table A2

Average Slopes (t-Statistics) from Annual Regressions of
Five-Year Stock Returns on Change in Shares and Selected Firm Characteristics
Variation in Treatment of Outliers

Intercept	Change in Shares	Book Market	Value- Glamor	Capital Invest.	Equity Assets	Log (Market)
Baseline: Fama-MacBeth, Outliers Set to One-Half Percentile						
16.11	-0.16	0.03	-1.24	-0.00	-0.00	0.58
(5.33)	(5.05)	(5.33)	(2.99)	(0.55)	(0.34)	(1.35)
No Correction for Outliers						
19.17	-0.13	0.01	-1.69	-0.00	0.01	0.40
(5.43)	(3.08)	(3.52)	(3.82)	(0.77)	(1.05)	(0.85)
Outliers Excluded						
15.28	-0.17	0.03	-1.08	-0.01	-0.00	0.60
(4.87)	(6.28)	(4.46)	(2.48)	(0.66)	(0.14)	(1.38)

Note: The variables are defined in table 1. The dependent variable is the five-year ex-post return (percent, AR) calculated from the end of April in the year following the change in shares and firm characteristics. The statistics reported for the Fama-MacBeth specification are the average coefficients from the nine annual cross-sectional regressions between 1983 and 1991 and the t-statistics are the average slopes divided by their time-series standard error. In the base case, for those variables subject to outliers--the book-to-market ratio, capital investment, and the equity-to-asset ratio, the outliers in excess of the top and bottom one-half percentile each year are set equal to the one-half percentile. In the regression with no correction for outliers, the outliers are included, while in the final regression the outliers are excluded from the analysis.

Appendix B: Use of the increment or decrement to funds resulting from the change in shares

When a firm issues shares it generates funds and when it repurchases shares it uses funds. In general, the increment or decrement to funds should be offset by a change in another balance sheet item. With regard to equity activity motivated by deviations of stock price from fundamental value, the use or source of funds is critical for the implications of the predictive power of the change in shares for economic welfare. If such changes in shares are generally offset by a change in other financial assets or liabilities, the implications for economic welfare are fairly modest, since the change just represents a reshuffling of financial variables. If, however, the changes in shares are offset by nonfinancial assets, specifically capital, then the economic welfare implications are quite large since they demonstrate an ability for noisy movements in stock prices to effect the distribution of capital.

In this paper, two reasons to issue or repurchase shares are considered other than the variation of stock price from fundamental value: a desire to normalize leverage, measured by the lagged equity-to-asset ratio; and a desire to change the size of the corporation, measured by the contemporaneous rate of capital investment. To some extent, these two reasons should also measure the use or source of funds generated by a change in shares motivated by the variation of stock price from fundamental value. For example, if firms pay down liabilities with proceeds from issuance motivated by an elevated stock price, then such changes in shares should have a profound effect on the equity-to-asset ratio and little effect on capital investment. Similarly, if firms acquire financial assets with the proceeds, the changes in shares should have a moderate effect on the equity-to-asset ratio and no effect on capital investment.

The results presented in table B1 address these issues by regressing the capital

38

investment rate and the change in the equity-to-asset ratio on the change in shares using OLS and then instrumenting for the change in shares with the book-to-market ratio and the value-glamor index. In so far as the instruments are proxies for deviations of stock price from fundamental value, the IV coefficient estimates measure the effect of changes in shares motivated by such deviation. The regressions also include both as independent variables and as instruments the log of market value and year dummies.

As can be seen in the table, the OLS estimates indicate that a one percent increase in shares is associated with a 0.1 percent increase in the equity-to-asset ratio. However, when the valuation variables are used as instruments, the coefficient rises to 0.2 percent, suggesting a greater tendency for liabilities to be the source of funds for repurchases or the use of funds for issues.

With regard to capital investment, the result is more dramatic. The OLS estimates find a one percentage point increase in the change in shares typically associated with a 0.4 percentage point increase in the capital investment rate. However, the IV estimates suggest an effect that is 9 times as large, 3.7 percentage points. On the face of it, the results suggest changes in shares motivated by the deviation of stock price from fundamental value have a significant effect on capital investment.

There are reasons to be skeptical of this result. The proxies for the deviation of stock price from fundamental value are also good proxies for the marginal profitability of capital. Even if capital investment were influenced by valuation-motivated changes in shares, it seems highly likely that the initial offset would be seen in financial variables. At most, what this exercise may have identified is what Loughran and Ritter (1997) call "confounding effects," managers and investors simultaneously over or understate the corporations' prospects, leading capital investment to correlate with stock price deviations from fundamental value. In this case, the deviations from fundamental value would not necessarily be influencing capital investment, although they would be indicative of systematic mistakes in the decisions of managers that would tend to decrease economic welfare.

Table B1

Regressions Examining Funding Use of Change in Shares
OLS, and with Change in Shares Instrumented for With
Book/Market, Value-Glamor Index, and Market Value

Estimation Technique	Dependent Variable	Intercept	Change in Shares	Market Value	R^2
OLS	Change in Equity/ Assets	-2.28 (7.00)	0.11 (22.33)	0.11 (3.48)	0.02
IV	Change in Equity/ Assets	-2.84 (7.81)	0.23 (7.04)	0.19 (4.93)	0.004
OLS	Capital Investment	36.00 (26.44)	0.43 (20.44)	-1.13 (8.70)	0.02
IV	Capital Investment	19.50 (9.58)	3.73 (20.84)	1.37 (6.20)	0.02

Note: The variables are defined in table 1. T-statistics are in parentheses. The regressions include time dummies (not shown) and time dummies are also included as instruments.

References

Asquith, Paul and David W. Mullins, 1986, Equity issues and offering dilution, *Journal of Financial Economics* 15, 61-89.

Berk, Jonathan B., 1995, A critique of size-related anomalies, *The Review of Financial Studies* 8, 275-286.

Dann, Larry, 1981, Common stock repurchases: An analysis of returns to bondholders and stockholders, *Journal of Financial Economics* 9, 115-138.

Fama, Eugene F. and J. MacBeth, 1973, Risk, return and equilibrium: Empirical tests, *Journal of Political Economy* 81, 607-636.

Fama, Eugene F. and Kenneth R. French, 1992, The cross-section of expected stock returns, *The Journal of Finance* 47, 427-465.

Ikenberry, David, Josef Lakonishok and Theo Vermaelen, 1995, Market underreaction to open market share repurchases, *Journal of Financial Economics* 39, 181-208.

Lakonishok, Josef, Andrei Shleifer, and Robert w. Vishny, 1994, Contrarian investment, extrapolation, and risk, *The Journal of Finance* 49, 1541-1578.

Loughran, Tim, and Jay R. Ritter, 1995, The new issues puzzle, *The Journal of Finance* 50, 23-51.

Loughran, Tim, and Jay R. Ritter, 1997, The operating performance of firms conducting seasoned equity offerings, *The Journal of Finance* 52, 1823-1850.

Masulis, Ron, 1980, Stock repurchase by tender offer: An analysis of common stock price changes, *Journal of Finance* 35, 305-318.

Masulis, Ron and A. N. Korwar, 1986, Seasoned equity offerings: an empirical investigation, *Journal of Financial Economics* 15, 91-118.

Mikkelson, W. H. and M. M. Partch, 1986, The valuation effects of security offerings and the issuance process, *Journal of Financial Economics* 15, 31-60.

Nelson, William R., 1999, Evidence of excess returns on firms that issue or repurchase equity, *Finance and Economics Discussion Series*, Federal Reserve Board, Washington D.C., (forthcoming).

Rosenfeld, A., 1982, Repurchase offers: Information adjusted premiums and shareholder's response, Working Paper, Purdue University.

Vermaelen, Theo, 1981, Common stock repurchases and market signalling, *Journal of Financial Economics* 9, 139-183.

_____, 1984, Repurchase tender offers, signalling and managerial incentives, *Journal of Financial and Quantitative Analysis* 19, 163-183.